The Prison Poems of Ho Chi Minh

The Prison Poems of Ho Chi Minh

with photographs and introduction by

Larry Towell

Cormorant Books

Copyright © photographs, Larry Towell, 1992

Published with the assistance of the Canada Council, and the Ontario Arts Council.

The translation of Ho Chi Minh's poems was originally published in *Prison Diary* at Foreign Languages Publishing House in Hanoi, the Socialist Republic of Vietnam, and was printed at Tien Bo Press. The translations are by Dang The Binh.

Some of this material previously appeared in *This Magazine* and *Border Crossings*.

Published by Cormorant Books Inc.,
RR 1, Dunvegan, Ontario, Canada K0C 1J0.

Printed and bound in Canada.

Canadian Cataloguing in Publication Data

    Ho, Chi Minh, 1890-1969

        The prison poems of Ho Chi Minh

    Translation from the Vietnamese.
    ISBN 0-920953-86-7

        I. Towell, Larry II. Dang, The Binh III. Title

    PL4378.9.H5P7313 1992 895.9'223 C92-090402-5

國忠大龍
為見點真
或始優出
去時愁門
出頭憂竹
人过有開
囚患人籠

INTRODUCTION

July 1946, Paris *

President Ho Chi Minh had led a Vietnamese delegation to France to negotiate national independence and venues for a unified North and South Vietnam. At a press conference in the Royal Monceau's reception room on the River Seine, he was being heckled by a journalist.

"Mr. President, you are a Communist, aren't you?"
"Yes."
"Have you been in the Resistance?"
"Yes."
"How long?"
"About forty years."
"Have you been in prison too?"
"Yes."
"What prison?"
"Many, sir."
"Long?"
The reply given in French came unexpectedly... "In prison, time is always long."

---

* These negotiations, provided for in the Preliminary Agreements of March 6 of that year, gave birth to the Fontainebleau conference near Paris. Unfortunately, French colonialists torpedoed the agreements and the nationwide resistance against the French broke out on December 19, 1946, ending in July 1954 with the Dien Bien Phu victory for Vietnam. French withdrawal was superseded by U.S. combat forces which resulted in one of the longest and most barbaric wars in modern history. The American war with Vietnam ended in 1973 with a U.S. withdrawal.

August 1942, Asia

The second year of World War II was drawing to a close. The Japanese had taken possession of Indo-China, but in Vietnam, rebel forces had emerged and were firmly established in the uplands.

Near the Sino-Vietnamese border, Kuomintang police had just arrested a man about whom they knew nothing, except that he called himself Ho Chi Minh. He claimed to be a representative of the Vietnamese patriots on his way to confer with Chiang Kai-shek regarding a common front of Vietnamese and Chinese people against the Japanese.

The man before them was dressed simply. His manner was unusual and his demeanour self-confident. He had studied in the U.S. and in Europe and he spoke perfect Chinese. As Vietnam and China had been enemies for 2000 years, he was instantly committed to irons.

As the stars faded in the pre-dawn, Ho Chi Minh was sent on a lead with hands bound. In front of him, a pig was being carried by two guards. At nightfall, as silent birds returned to their nests, he was forced into a makeshift jail near a rubbish pile, with one leg shackled in such a way as to avoid sleeping on the latrine edge.

First he was brought to the Tsingsi jail; then he was taken to Nanning; from Nanning he was sent to Kweilin, and from Kweilin to Luichow where he began to retrace his circuitous steps across southern China. Surviving the most difficult conditions, and often in leg irons, he criss-crossed thirteen districts of Kwangsi province and was confined in thirty prefecture and district prisons for a total of thirteen months.

Chinese jails were notoriously disease-ridden and abominable. In spite of the deprivation of food, water and light, however, inmates lived a rather family-like existence. Sometimes in the darkness of the cell, Ho Chi Minh observed his companions asleep and awake, innocent-faced men surrounded by bugs like "tanks on manoeuvres", with mosquitoes "attacking in squadrons". Or he would awaken beside someone who had starved to death. The world was at war while he languished in irons. At such moments as these, he opened a worn notebook and jotted down his impressions of the day.

This prisoner wrote in the language of his jailers who would have been suspicious of anything written in Vietnamese. Finally, in the late autumn of 1943, he was released from custody in Liuchow. Little more than a skeleton, he took the long road back to the frontier, his diary still in hand.

This is the origin of a hundred-odd classically composed quatrains and T'ang poems written in Chinese. All are sketches from life in the prison and are translated here by Dang The Binh.

The Photographs

The human cost of U. S. involvement against Ho Chi Minh's War of Independence was staggering.

Over four million U. S. citizens served in what has been called America's "national descent into evil". The average age of the U. S. infantry was nineteen. More than 58,000 died and 300,000 were wounded. An estimated 2000 are listed as "missing in action". One eighth of those who served suffer from Post Traumatic Stress Disorder (PTSD), a psychological syndrome caused by the guilt, the trauma, and the rejection upon their return. Many remain unable to sustain jobs or enjoy normal familial relationships. More veterans have committed suicide since the war ended than were killed in combat (an estimated 110,000). As many as a third of the prisoners in U. S. penitentiaries are Vietnam vets, as are a large percentage of the homeless males who roam American streets. Others live a life of disassociation and irrelevancy in the backwoods areas of California, Oregon, Hawaii, and Washington State, for society neither wants nor cares for them.

America lost militarily and morally, but it was a tragedy of physical and epic dimension for those whose homeland remains one of the most impoverished places on earth. Although Vietnamese authorities have never published figures, an estimated 600,000 North Vietnamese soldiers died in the struggle. Two to three million persons were killed in total, and as many again were wounded and maimed—10% of the entire population. Ten thousand have since died due to left-over land mines and over 100,000 are still "missing in action". An unknown number of infant bodies continue to be born misshapen from Agent Orange. Others are doomed to die from cancer due to wartime chemical residues in water and fields. Perhaps one of the saddest legacies of the war is the 25,000 to 50,000 Amerasians, the offspring of U. S. GIs and Vietnamese women. Ostracized in their own country, they eke out a living on the streets begging or selling black-market wares and cigarettes. International observers estimate that between six and seven million Vietnamese are slowly dying of starvation and diseases caused from malnutrition because food and other supplies cannot be produced or imported in sufficient quantities as the U. S. continues a crippling wartime embargo. The Vietnam war never has ended. The cycle of vengeance continues to click . . . spin . . . click.

September 1990

Eight U.S. Vietnam veterans travel to Yen Vien, near Hanoi, to rebuild a health clinic that had been destroyed in the indiscriminate 1972 Christmas bombings. They had privately raised the $30,000 for re-construction and will be working side-by-side with former enemies from the North and old allies from the South. The vets would be hosted by the Yen Vien People's Committee.

Half of the team suffers from PTSD. It is believed that helping the Vietnamese to rebuild their clinic will aid in the psychological recovery of the Americans, replacing bad memories with good, thus coming full circle with the war. It also seems inevitable that such projects will assist in the healing of international relations.

The vets are operating under the auspices of the Veterans Vietnam Restoration Project (VVRP), a private California-based organization seeking political and social action as a means of redressing their past and of restoring their present.

The VVRP was formed in 1988, inspired by the example of ex-Vietnam veteran S. Brian Willson who, in September 1987, while protesting the shipment of weapons to the Nicaraguan contras, was run over by a munitions train in northern California, losing both of his legs on the tracks. The formation and objectives of the VVRP were initially opposed by the U.S. State Department.

As the veterans board the plane at the San Francisco Airport, U.S.-led coalition forces are preparing for the Persian Gulf War to, according to President George Bush, "put Vietnam behind our backs once-and-for-all." The paradox was painful. Whose backs? Which *our*? Whose Vietnam?

The vets, confronted by a new eagerness for conflict in the American psyche, fight valiantly on TV and radio. Their return is overshadowed in New York by a camouflaged General Norman

Schwarzkopf being paraded under tons of cascading tickertape and confetti. U.S. magazines declared him to be the "sexiest man in America."

Hanoi, September 17

School children, with small book bags, uncoil from a stick the national flag of Vietnam, chanting in unison, "Uncle Ho! Uncle Ho!" Its five-pointed star hangs limp in a dead wind. John Baca takes a boy's bronze-coloured hand and runs it over the scars of his stomach. In 1970, he had thrown himself onto a live grenade, attempting to smother it with his body.

The child, at first frightened by the massive and disfiguring scar, begins to poke at the rolls of flesh and cauterized tissue. The construction crew of Americans and Vietnamese soon circle to stare at the emotionally-packed phenomenon. John, lacking language, is attempting to share his own suffering in recognition of theirs.

Water-buffalo wade through the lotus flowers that float on a lake man-made by a B-52. The superbomb had missed its target and landed in a rice paddy, its arms stretched sacrificially skyward to receive it. Conical hats float on the water from the heads of women whose bodies are totally submerged in search of aquatic snails. They surface periodically for air. The sun passes its fingers through the hairs of water on a lake of floating hats.

The photographs were taken over a period of three weeks in North Vietnam. I spent mornings at the Yen Vien work-site and afternoons roaming the streets of Hanoi taking photographs, as the spirit led, through the alleys, the rice paddies, the hospitals, markets, fields, and cemeteries. I photographed the U.S. vets with their Vietnamese hosts, and I photographed the national heroes—the paraplegic and quadriplegic North Vietnamese vets. Always above them hung the portrait of Ho Chi Minh like a crucifix in an Irish kitchen. Offering what? His hand. Beckoning intensely.

Ho, whose real name was Nguyen Sinh Cung, was born in 1890 in a small village in central Vietnam. His father was a farm labourer and a prostitute's son who had managed to rise to the rank of mandarin through his own assiduous study. Nguyen Sinh Sac eventually left the imperial court in Hue abandoning his wife and children to travel the country as an itinerant medicine man and teacher.

At an early age, Ho Chi Minh inherited his father's wanderlust, but on a grander scale. He travelled the globe for decades as a solitary soul. He never married and seldom contacted kin. He became affiliated with the Communist Party in Paris in the 1920's, obsessed with the fate of his country and its dream of independence. As a playwright, a freelance journalist, a pursuer of debating societies, a cook, a communist agent, and a revolutionary, he used many aliases in his life, the last of which was Ho Chi Minh.

He became the unique and inscrutable leader who somehow managed to hold the power of American military technology at bay in a David-and-Goliath struggle unprecedented in our time. His sandals were cut from discarded auto tires. He lived in spartan stable quarters behind the former French Governor General's Palace in Hanoi. He drank tea with visitors, presenting the ladies with a rose, and the men with an ironic joke. Ho Chi Minh possessed all the elements of myth and legend. Of this, he was by no means unaware . . . .

Although his inner essence and private life have remained a mystery, we have been left with one rice paper clue. His prison poems, numbering one hundred and fifteen in total, capture the smallest nuances of his prison life of lice hunts, scabies, thievery, starvation, the cruelty of wardens and fetters, the cold, discomfort and stench which he conquered with the song of birds at dawn, the morning sun, or the face of a prisoner "now all smiles". He made poems containing "verses of steel" for poets who "should form a front line of attack".

I walk the Long Binh Bridge across the Red River to Hanoi. Overhead, massive beams twist and rust in the air—the evidence of B-52 anger. It is an hour's walk to Ho Chi Minh's mausoleum where his mummified remains lie resting on exhibit. Who is this man displayed now like dried fruit under glass? Today I'd seen his face everywhere—in private homes and dining rooms, in a school mural and in a street barber shop. Why this reverence? To both young and old he is "Uncle Ho". Why this affection?

In post-revolutionary Nicaragua, I'd seen Sandino's silhouette painted across the length and breadth of each rock face and fence like a poor man's flag. Ho Chi Minh too seemed to be in the bones of a nation by painful birth. By contrast, I reflected on my own Sir John A. MacDonald. National hero? Idealist? Democratic visionary? Sure. But Canada has slipped into independence like a silk glove. Could I picture John A. as a guerilla combatant? Tortured? Assassinated? Could I picture him writing poems—and why the *Sir*?

Ho Chi Minh was a nationalist, a Marxist, an idealist, an admirer of U.S. Presidents Jefferson and Lincoln, a believer in democracy, and a classical poet. Perhaps his followers have turned out to be of a more authoritarian mould. But perhaps, if Vietnam could enjoy the sheer luxury of time to heal, this would not be so.

The photographs represent Vietnam as it felt to me. They are here presented with the quintessential Ho Chi Minh.

Larry Towell

*Larry Towell would like to thank the Canada Council
and the Ontario Arts Council for their financial assistance,
Phan Nhuan for his introductory research,
and his wife Ann for her encouragement.
He also thanks the people of the Socialist Republic of Vietnam
who opened their doors everywhere
and the Foreign Language Publishing House in Hanoi
which first introduced the diary in its entirety.*

IDEOGRAMS ANALYSED

Freed, the prisoner can build the country.
Misfortunes are tests of a man's loyalty.
To worry about the common good is a great merit no doubt.
Let the prison door open and the real dragon will fly out.

The poem written in Chinese ideograms:

囚　人　出　去　或　為　國
患　过　頭　時　始　見　忠
人　有　憂　愁　優　點　大
籠　開　竹　門　出　真　龍

The analysis:

Take 人 (man) from 囚 (prison),
add 或 (probability) and you get 國 (country).
Lop off the top of 患 (misfortune),
that gives 忠 (loyalty).
Add 人 (man) to 憂 (worry) to get 優 (merit).
Take 竹 (bamboo) off the top of 籠 (cell),
that leaves 龍 (dragon).

BEGINNING THE DIARY

I've never been given to chanting verse;
But what else can a captive do in jail?
These long days I'll spend composing poems:
Singing may ease the wait for freedom.

EVENING

The meal over, the sun sinks below the western horizon.
From all corners rise folk tune and people's song.
Suddenly this dismal, gloomy Zingsi prison
Is turned into a little music academy.

OVERNIGHT STOP AT LUNGQUAN

All day my two horses* have trotted, tireless.
When night comes I'm served with five-spice chicken.**
Bed-bugs and cold draughts attack, merciless.
How welcome, the dawn song of the golden oriole!

*Jokingly, the two legs

**To cook this dish, the legs of the chichen are tied crosswise. A jocular description of the way the prisoner's limbs are bound at night.

GODE PRISON

Life in the ward needs some kind of housekeeping:
Wood, rice, oil, salt—everything must be bought and paid for.
In front of each cell a little stove stands
On which rice and broth boil all day.

THE STOCKS

I

Opening a hungry mouth like a wicked monster,
Each night the stocks seize the ankles of the prisoner.
Their jaws grip the right leg of the wretch;
Only the left is free to bend and stretch.

II

There happen in this world things even stranger:
People jostle to get their feet in first.
For once locked in there's some hope of peaceful slumber;
Otherwise, where to lie tranquil on this crowded ground?

EVENING SCENERY

A rose blossoms, and then fades.
It blooms and withers heedlessly.
But its sweetness the prison cells pervades
To arouse our deepfelt bitterness.

MORNING

Every morning the sun, rising over the wall,
Beams on the gate, but the gate is not yet open.
Inside the prison lingers a gloomy pall,
But we know that outside the sun has risen.

THE MORNING SUN

The morning sun into the prison penetrates:
The smoke clears away, the mist dissipates.
The breath of life suddenly fills the skies,
And the prisoners' faces are now all smiles.

THE CHARGES

Sixty cents to get a pot of rice cooked.
A basin of hot water costs no less than one yuan.
For sixty cents' worth of goods you're charged a full yuan:
How clearly the prices in prison are fixed!

LIGHTING COSTS

For the cost of lighting each newcomer pays:
Six yuan *per person in local coin.*
In this realm of darkness and haze
Light is worth only that much money.

TUNGZHENG

Tungzheng jail can be compared to Pingma:
Each meal a bowl of gruel, the stomach as good as empty.
But water and light we can have aplenty,
And each day for airing the cells are twice opened.

THE "INN"

Newcomers to the prison, as a rule,
Must spend the night beside the privy.
Anyone who wants to sleep peacefully
To pay some cash let him be ready!

GUARDS CARRY A PIG

I

Going with us, guards carry a pig
On their shoulders, while I am rudely dragged along.
A man is treated worse than a pig,
Once he's deprived of his liberty.

II

Of the thousand sources of bitterness and sorrow
None can be worse than the loss of liberty.
Even in word and gesture, you're no longer free:
They just haul you along, like horse or buffalo.

COLD NIGHT

In the cold autumn night, with neither quilt nor mattress
I curl myself up for warmth but cannot close my eyes.
Moonlight on the banana-palms adds to the chill.
I look through the bars: the Little Bear has lain down in the skies.

GOOD-BYE TO A TOOTH

You were, my friend, hard and unyielding;
Not like the tongue, soft and sinuous.
The bitter and the sweet we have shared till now,
But this day each of us must go his way.

TRANSFERRED TO TIANBAO ON "DOUBLE TEN"* DAY

Every house is decked with lanterns and flowers:
It's national day, the whole country is filled with delight.
But this is the moment I am put in chains for transfer:
Contrary winds continue to hamper the eagle's flight.

DUSK

To the wood seeking shelter a bird flies, forlorn.
Leisurely a lone cloud floats across wide heaven.
In yonder mountain hamlet a girl is grinding corn.
The grain ground, a hot fire glows red in the oven.

*Tenth of October, the Chinese National Day under the Kuomintang regime.

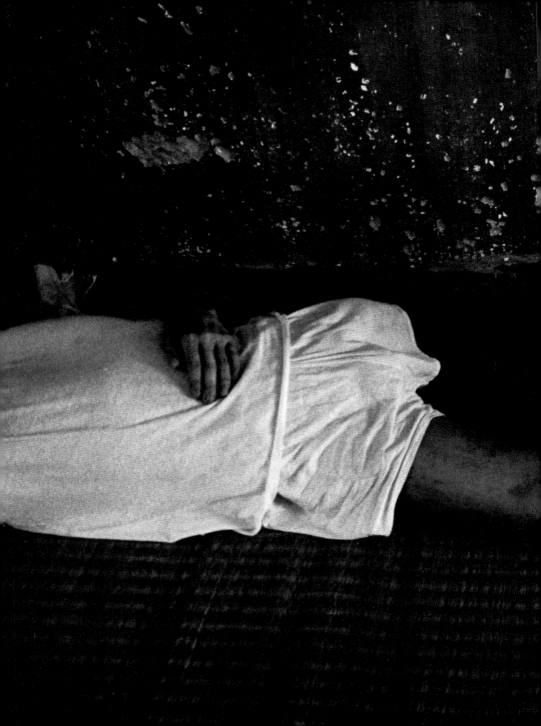

HARD IS THE ROAD OF LIFE

I

Having travelled over steep mountain and deep ravine,
How could I expect in the plain to meet even greater danger?
In the mountain I suffered no harm from the tiger;
In the plain I met with men and was thrown in jail.

II

I am a delegate of the Vietnamese people
On his way to China to meet a high official.
Why should a storm break out over a peaceful scene
And I be flung in prison for hospitality?

III

A loyal man, with my heart torn by no remorse,
I'm somehow suspected of being a Chinese traitor.
It has never been easy in life to steer one's course,
But how difficult it all has become now!

DEPARTURE BEFORE DAWN

I

The cocks have crowed only once: night is not yet passed.
With a retinue of stars the moon sails high over the mountain tops.
On the road the traveller has set out for a long journey,
His face is beaten again and again by gusts of the autumn blast.

II

Pale east turns rosy, widening day.
The last shades of night have swept away.
A warm breath blows over measureless skies,
And the wayfaring poet feels happiness rise.

ON THE ROAD

My arms and legs are tightly bound.
But in the hills birds sing and flowers blossom.
Who can stop my pleasure in sweetness of scent and sound?
In my long trudge I may feel a little less lonesome.

SCABIES

Blotched red and blue as though dressed in brocade;
Scratching all day you'd think we were playing the guitar.
As honoured guests, we make a parade of our rich attire.
Strange virtuosos, sharing an itch for music we surely are!

THE FLUTE
OF A FELLOW-PRISONER

Nostalgically a flute wails in the ward.
Sad grows the tone, mournful the melody.
Miles away, beyond passes and streams, in infinite melancholy,
A lonely figure mounts a tower gazing far and wide.

PRISON LIFE

A stove for each of the prison folk,
And earthen pots of every size,
For making tea, boiled vegetables, and rice:
All day the whole place is filled with smoke.

NO SMOKING

Here smoking is strictly prohibited!
Your tobacco by the warder is quickly confiscated.
Of course he can smoke his pipe whenever he wishes;
But just try to have a puff and he'll handcuff you.

THE WATER RATION

The water ration is half a basin only:
You can either wash or make tea, as you please.
If you want to clean your face, then go without your tea.
Should you be keen on tea, well, you can't wash your phiz.

ADVICE TO MYSELF

Without the cold and bleakness of winter
The warmth and splendour of spring could never be.
Misfortunes have steeled and tempered me
And even more strengthened my resolve.

?!

Forty days have gone by in useless misery,
Forty days and nights of ineffable suffering.
And now I'm being sent back to Liuzhou:
The prospect is deeply disheartening!

?!

Liuzhou, Guilin, and now again Liuzhou;
Kicked back and forth like a soccer ball.
Innocent, I've been dragged over Guangsi, to and fro:
For an end to this shuttling can one ever hope at all?

ARRIVAL AT TIANBAO JAIL

Today I have walked fifty-three kilometres.
My hat and clothes are soaking through, my shoes in tatters.
Without a place to sleep, all through the night
I sit by the edge of the latrine, waiting for light.

JAILED GAMBLERS

The State supplies no food to gamblers in jail
So they may quickly learn to mend their ways.
Each day "affluent" inmates can enjoy good eating.
As for the poor, hunger makes their eyes and mouths water.

A JAILED GAMBLER DIES

Nothing but skin and bone remained of him.
He slept close to my side only last night.
But misery, cold and hunger were the end of him,
And this morning gone he was to the world of eternal night.

THE PRESS:
WARM WELCOME TO WILLKIE*

Both good friends of China, for Zhongqing
Together we are heading.
But there you are, offered the seat of honour;
While here am I, down below, a prisoner.
Like you I'm a visiting delegate;
Why then is the difference in treatment such?
This is life: coldness to some, warmth towards others.
*For ever eastward flow the waters.***

*Head of an American delegation to China in 1942.

**Major Chinese rivers all flow east towards the sea.

LEARNING TO PLAY CHESS

I

To while the time away we learn to play chess.
Horse and foot are engaged in endless chase.
Move with lightning speed in attack or defence:
Talent and nimble feet will give you the upper hand.

II

Look far ahead and ponder deeply.
Be resolute: attack and attack incessantly.
A wrong move and even your two chariots* are useless;
Come the right juncture: a pawn can bring you success.

III

The forces on both sides are balanced equally,
But victory will come only to one player.
Advance, retreat—do both with unerring strategy:
Only then can you be called a great commander.

**The most powerful men on a Chinese chessboard.*

ENDLESS RAINS

Nine days of rain, of sunshine but one day:
Really the sky above has shown no feeling.
Tattered shoes, muddy road, legs caked in clay!
Still, endlessly we must keep slogging on.

IRONY

The State feeds me, I stop at State-owned palaces.
Guards work in relays to keep me company.
Passing by mounts and streams, I enjoy majestic views.
It fills a man with pride to be so privileged.

COUNTRY SCENE

When first I came here the rice was still tender green.
Now half the autumn harvest has already been brought in.
Everywhere peasants' faces wear smiles of gladness,
And the ricefields resound with songs of happiness.

LISTENING TO THE SOUND OF RICE-POUNDING

Under the pestle how terribly the rice suffers!
But it comes out of the pounding as white as cotton.
In this world the same process happens to humans:
Hard trials turn them into diamonds bright.

MR GUO

Like duckweed meeting water, glad we were to see each other.
How kind and cordial Mr Guo was to me!
Nothing much: "A little gift of coal in wintry weather."
Yet, that such people still exist is truly a blessing.

TO MY STAFF, STOLEN BY A GUARD

All your time with me you've been upright and unyeilding,
Hand in hand through many seasons, times of mist and snow.
Cursed be the rogue who caused our parting!
We'll grieve for each other for many a morrow.

TIANTUNG

For each meal only a bowl of rice gruel:
The hungry stomach moans, wails, and twists.
Three yuan *of rice is not enough to feed a man*
When wood sells as dear as cinnamon and rice as pearls.

SLEEPLESS NIGHTS

During the long and sleepless nights in prison,
I've written more than a hundred poems on thraldom.
Often at the end of a quatrain I put down my brush
And through the bars look up at the sky of freedom.

RESTRICTIONS

Without freedom one leads a wretched life!
Even on relieving nature restrictions are imposed.
When the door is opened the bowels, alas, aren't ready;
When one has the gripes, it remains of course closed.

PERMITTED TO TAKE A WALK IN THE PRISON YARD

After such long disuse my legs are soft like cotton.
Trying a few steps, I stagger and totter.
But very soon bellows the chief-warder:
"Hey you, come back, no loitering in prison!"

WRITING A PETITION
FOR JAIL-MATES

Being in the same boat, how could I refuse to help you?
On your behalf to the authorities I wrote a petition.
"Whereas ... in consequence of ... "
                    —For such newly-learned jargon
No end of thanks I got as my due.

IN A BOAT
TO YONGNING (Nanning)

Borne by the current, the boat floats towards Yongning.
My legs are lashed to the rail, a new style of hanging!
On both river banks a prosperous countryside:
In midstream light fishing-boats swiftly glide.

THE ROAD-MENDER

Drenched with rain, flogged by the wind, resting never:
Road-mender, in what wretched conditions you work!
Of all who pass—on foot, on horseback, or in a carriage—
How many will show you their gratitude ever?

TWILIGHT

The wind hones its sword on the mountain rocks.
The boughs of trees are pierced with the spears of the cold.
The bell from a far-off pagoda hastens the traveller's steps.
Slowly the flute-playing buffalo-boys ride home to the villages.

MOONLIGHT

In jail there is neither flower nor wine.
What could one do when the night is so exquisite?
To the window I go and look at the moonshine.
Through the bars the moon gazes at the poet.

COMMOTION IN VIETNAM

News reports in the Nanning press

Death rather than servitude! Everywhere in my country
The flags of insurrection once more proudly flutter.
Oh, how sad at such a time to be a prisoner:
To rush into battle I wish I could be free!

SADNESS

The whole world is ablaze with the flames of war.
Fighters eagerly ask to be sent to the front.
In jail inaction weighs on the prisoner heavier still:
His noble ambitions are not worth a paltry cent.

AIR-RAID WARNING

November 12

Enemy planes come roaring in the sky.
People flee helter-skelter, leaving the place empty.
Out of prison we are ordered for safety:
How gladly we all hasten to comply!

THE ELEVENTH OF NOVEMBER

I

Formerly when came the Eleventh of November,
Of the armistice in Europe the anniversary was observed.
Today bloody fighting rages the five continents over:
The wicked Nazis for this crime must bear the blame.

II

Now China has been resisting for almost six years.
Her heroic feats of arms are known all the world over.
Although victory is just around the corner,
When the time comes for counter-offensive more effort is required.

III

All over Asia anti-Japanese flags flutter.
Big flags, little flags—in size they differ.
Of course the big banners must be present;
But the little ones should never be wanting.

FOUR MONTHS HAVE PASSED

"One day within prison walls seems as long
*　　　　　　　　　　as a thousand years without."*
How right the ancients were, no doubt!
Four months of a subhuman life, it appears,
Have aged me even more than a dozen years.

Indeed
> *For four months I've lived on meagre fare;*
> *For four months I've never had sound sleep;*
> *For four months I've never changed my wear;*
> *For four months I've never had a dip.*

And so
> *One of my teeth has fallen away;*
> *Much of my hair has turned white and grey;*
> *Scabies covers the whole of my body;*
> *I'm dark and thin like a hungry demon.*

Fortunately
> *Stubborn and persevering,*
> *I've not yielded an inch.*
> *Physically I'm suffering,*
> *But my spirit will never flinch.*

READING THE "ANTHOLOGY OF A THOUSAND POETS"

Of nature the ancients loved to sing the charms:
Moon and flowers, snow and wind, mist, hills and streams.
But in our days poems should contain verses of steel,
And poets should form a front line for attack.

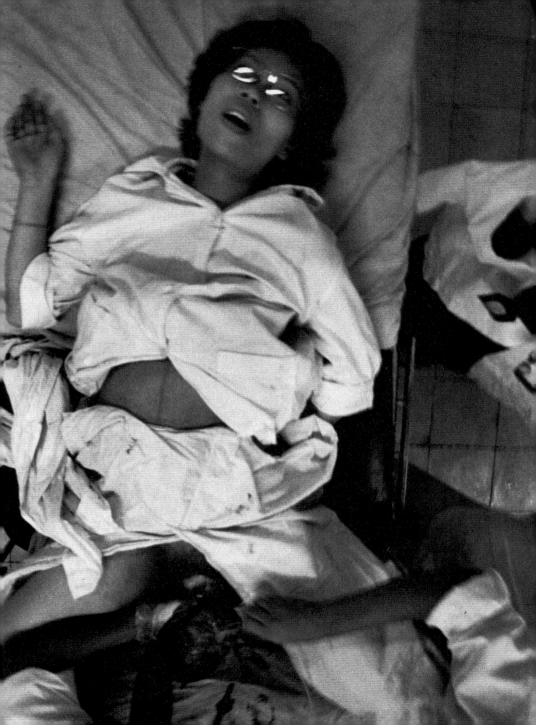

ON THE WAY TO NANNING

The supple rope has been replaced with hard irons.
At every step like bracelets of jade they jingle.
Although a prisoner, held suspect of spying,
Mine is the dignified bearing of a Court official.

REGRET AT TIME LOST

On a militant an adverse destiny maintains its hold.
Eight useless months now have I spent in chains.
One day is worth a thousand taels of gold:
When can I ever hope to be free again?

AUTUMN NIGHT

At the gate guards holding their rifles stand.
Above them shredded clouds are drifting with the moon.
Bed-bugs swarm about like tanks manoeuvring.
Like air squadrons, mosquitoes regroup and disperse.
My heart travels a thousand li *to my country.*
Sadness twists my dreams into a thousand tangled skeins.
An innocent man, yet I've been a whole year in chains.
With tears dropping on my inkslab, I make another poem on captivity.

THE WEATHER IS CLEARING UP

Everything evolves, such is the law of nature.
After days of rain, here's fine weather coming!
In an instant the earth has cast off its damp clothing;
Over ten thousand li the land spreads its mantle of brocade.,
Under warm sun and balmy wind flowers smile with rapture;
In the tall trees and shining boughs birds rehearse their trills.
Joy fills man's heart as well as the universe.
After bitter comes the sweet: so runs the course of nature.

August 29, 1942
September 10, 1943

AFTER PRISON, PRACTISING MOUNTAIN-CLIMBING*

The mountains embrace the clouds, the clouds hug the mountains.
The river below shines like a spotless mirror.
On the slopes of the Western Range, my heart beats as I wander,
Looking towards the Southern skies and thinking of old friends.

*After his release Ho Chi Minh took long walks in the mountains to recover his health.

SLEEPLESS NIGHT

The first watch . . . the second . . . the third watch fades.
I toss about, restless: sleep will not come, it seems.
The fourth watch . . . the fifth . . . No sooner have I closed my eyes
The five-pointed star is there to haunt my dreams.*

*The national flag of the Democratic Republic of Vietnam, founded by President Ho Chi Minh in 1915, is red with a five-pointed golden star

INDEX OF PHOTOS
All photos taken 1990.

cover photo:	Yen Vien worksite, Yen Vien.
pages 18-19:	Yen Vien
page 23:	Quan Su Buddist Monastery, Hanoi
pages 26-27:	U.S. vet John Baca with work crew and children, Yen Vien worksite
pages 30-31:	YenVien worksite
pages 36-37:	Thuan Thanh Centre for disabled Vietnamese vets, Habac Province
pages 40-41:	North Vietnam vet, Thuan Thanh Centre, Habac Province
pages 42-43:	North Vietnam vet, Thuan Thanh Centre, Habac Province
pages 48-49:	North Vietnam vet toasting friendship, Thuan Thanh Centre, Habac Province
page 53:	U.S. veteran Art James with North Vietnam vet, Thuan Thanh Centre, Habac Province
pages 54-55:	Benh Vien Tam Than psychiatric hospital, Hanoi
pages 56-57:	Benh Vien Tam Than psychiatric hospital, Hanoi
pages 64-65:	fields, Hanoi area
page 67:	fields, Hanoi area
pages 68-69:	fields, Hanoi area
pages 72-73:	fields, Hanoi area
pages 74-75:	fields, Hanoi area
pages 80-81:	Hanoi
page 85:	funeral, Hanoi
pages 88-89:	Van Vien Cemetery, Hanoi
pages 90-91:	Van Vien Cemetery, Hanoi
pages 94-95:	Van Vien Cemetery, Hanoi
page 97:	Hospital for mothers and newborns, Hanoi
pages 98-99:	Hospital for mothers and newborns, Hanoi
pages 104-105:	Hanoi
pages 106-107:	Hanoi
page 109:	Yen Vien worksite, Yen Vien

... Embroiled against colonial France, Vietnam was beleaguered by Japanese and besieged by U. S. combat forces, and invaded by its neighbours, China and Cambodia. For the past fifty years, world powers both large and small have attempted to crush the simplicity of Ho Chi Minh's dream.

These sixty-one quatrains and T'ang poems, composed during Ho's incarceration by the Chinese, reveal the political legend as a poet-philosopher in the great Asian tradition. They are here presented with images of contemporary Vietnam by MAGNUM photographer Larry Towell.

Larry Towell is the author of two books of poetry and an oral history on the Nicaraguan war. His photographs have been exhibited internationally and his photo-stories have been published in *LIFE* Magazine, *The New York Times Magazine,* and the British *Independent.* He lives on a small family farm in Ontario with his wife and three children. Larry has been associated with MAGNUM, the internationally celebrated co-operative of photo-journalists, since 1988.